In | Direction

ALVIN GREENBERG

In/Direction

DAVID R. GODINE · BOSTON

David R. Godine, Publisher
Boston, Massachusetts

★

A Godine Poetry Chapbook
Third Series

for Wendy Parrish
1950–1977

These miracles we did; but now, alas,
All measure and all language I should pass,
Should I tell what a miracle she was.

John Donne, "The Relic"

'But the way is dangerous, the
passage doubtful, the voyage
not thoroughly known.'

Mr. Richard Wilkes,
gent. (in Hakluyt,
Voyages & Discoveries)

1.

what we begin with is a ticket which reads: 'all the way.'
all the way down, all the way to the end . . . just all
      the way.
it does not read: feel free to wake up from this whenever
      you please.

*

we assume, even as we ask our way, that the oracle is mad:
'divinely mad,' of course. by what other device can we
      be spun
outward than by the gyroscope of such madness? either

the oracle madly whirls or the whole world teeters. nor,
in the midst of such presence, such fierce direction,
can the steps to knowledge be climbed, except we go
      down.

*

anger pops the plane windows at thirty thousand feet
and we are all sucked out into this dizzy vacuum,
victims—all of us—of the crash landing,

of the sudden derailment at horseshoe bend,
of the great liners colliding in the fog-bound harbor,
of chain accidents on the rain-slicked freeways
and screams and gunfire at midnight border crossings,

of tainted egg salad in the greyhound bus station,
of the washed-out bridge and the pebble in the shoe.

*

can we survive the myths of heroic voyagers? how shall
        we read
father's story of stowing away on a greek freighter to
        shanghai?
what museums did he visit? to whom did he send
        postcards?

do we have aging siblings who eat fish and rice every day?
how many years did it take him to find his way back to
        the family?
why does the oracle refuse to answer these all-important
        questions?

*

only at night are the borders open to this dark place called
'why we dream'—where only the crash, not the plane,
        can take us,

where guards replace our delicate passport photos with
        mirrors
and move like dali through our penetrable luggage.
        moneychangers
change our money, into water, into wine, and we are
        buried under

a shower of golden exports, deadly and necessary as our
        lives.

*

midnight is the point of embarcation: dark night of
    travel where
the tacky vaporetto steams into the intricate waterway
    where
the still surface reflects only the new moon, the old
    boat, where

nothing explains anything else: is to see double to see
    clearly?
must every journey be as dark as this? those would-be
    travelers,
awaiting their passports, do not think so—but they will
    learn:

they want the brightly painted boat that leaves at dawn,
    they want
lunch served by waiters in white coats and the far shore
    by dusk.
they have examined the schedules in the papers. well,
    then . . .

*

the journey itself is an arc, strenuous as one of those sunsets
that lasts for many hours and green as the greenest mirage,
but stone. a granite arch. we gather deckchairs beneath it,

reading our homer and marco polo, our hakluyt, our swift.
even on unbelievers we inflict the curve of our sky. it glows.

there is a little spinning in the distance, called night.

9

*

in the first dream of the intricate path, we walk back down
the long street, between the neighbors' sprinklers, to knock
at the door of my childhood. but who is this woman who
        lets us in,

whose children are having a party where no one we know
        is invited?
let us leave, quickly, this fiesta of strange cakes and ices.
leave quickly and not return. no one *i* know lives here
        anymore.

*

nothing useless, though, nothing that shouldn't be taken
        along
or bought as soon as offered. no such thing as excess
        baggage
or the tattered accumulations of all the places we've
        come from.

no need to abandon the primrose clinging to the railroad
        embankment
or the meadowlark calling out the boundaries of its small
        field,
that last half-acre that remains behind the new bolt
        factory,

or the factory, the tracks, the faded warning—'junction
        6oo ft.'
everywhere we have ever walked things come together
        like this,

and everything that ever was or is goes forward with us
    now.

*

we want to leave quick footprints in the snow
with such discretion that the trackers seeking our tracks
exclaim, 'we can't even tell which way they point,

the length of the stride indicates flight . . . or pursuit'
and even after the snow has melted, as it finally does,
the prints remain, still visible on quiet afternoons.

2.

now: turn off the motors and listen to the pure hum of
      motion.
remember: this tone which deepens as it spirals away into
      our dreams
is the intricate murmur of the past receding at the speed
      of life.

*

dreaming of how we lived among the cliff dwellers we fall
      once more.
our hands slip from the polished rungs of their steep
      buildings.
we cannot even grab each other. our slides show all the
      empty spaces

beneath which we lie fallen. dark as the night when we
      lost our way
among the intricate dreams of the tunnel diggers, these
      crumpled
forms are us, which breathe and rise. ok. picture more
      marvels yet.

*

some are devoured by their own maps of hunger, driven by
the illegible line on the passport where the expiration
      date goes;
they scramble toward the daylight of somewhere else,
      and what

can the ordinary traveler, oracle, or dreamer say to
      that, for whom

hope and motion are synonyms, like passion and
        direction, like
their bodies gliding across this line of possible identities.

*

swirling down these buried, invisible maps of the past,
paddles swept over, torrents spinning us around upon
        ourselves
in the amazing rush toward sea level, as if it were an ideal:

this is what we used to mean by 'water seeks its own level.'
such a crude physics informs our lives:
see how the lakes and rivers all descend upon one another.

*

today we have crossed the borders—unharmed,
        welcomed—
arrived among these unspeakable and most human
people who do as well as they mean.

shall we have commerce with such fierce practitioners?
shall their children run their fingers through our hair?
shall those who mean to devour us do so quickly?

*

when meeting strangers, regard the thumb of the major
        hand.
does it leap away from the fingers? distance is everything:
hurry! does it hide in the palm? make note of all the exits,

13

watch the mirrors, never never sit with your back to the
  door,
where is the lightswitch? don't even untie your shoes

unless the thumb bends outward, at the tip, like a
  sunflower.

*

we are away, now, on the dream of the white birch in a
  wooden tub
held high in the arms of the giant oak at dawn, the dream
that began with the escape of the threatened child, the
  dream

in which the oracle sent me to ransom my travel pictures—
i paid for them, i paid for them: though i hadn't even
  left yet!—
then ordered the car, pointed the way, and said, 'you
  drive.'

*

sooner or later we come to the dry parts. the dessicated
  guide,
who has drunk nothing in all these passages, cannot speak
the language of our needs. we've been told where the old
  wells are

but the old wells are dry. is this also called 'death by
  water,'

14

time to dream flash floods, dives from the cliff into the
      harbor?
the guide opens his mouth for direction and blue water
      spills out.

*

in dali's vision of turner's view of the harbor at duluth
the two sleek ocean liners rush to embrace each other,
the city bursts darkly uphill like an evening hurricane,

and in the twin mirrors of art and travel, dense with snow,
we are surprised at how much we resemble ourselves.
the weather's different here: beware of your friend, friend.

*

everything there is to see in these parts we've already seen.
we have pinned down maps with our out-turned thumbs,
      ridden
the deepest underground, consulted the knowledgeable.
      we have

been taken on lengthy tours of the great emotional desert,
      which
was no different than where i grew up, and visited the
      dream museum,
its galleries always dense with the same surprises. what
      next?

will we sample the boredom that unseasons the most
      exotic cuisine?

will we learn how they torture explorers here? see: i am
    already
buried up to my neck in myself under the hot sun of
    perception.

3.

the need for 'white space' leads us to the glacier, to the
    desert,
to the island lost in the faded waters of the south pacific
where we immediately trust the mss of our aloneness to
    the sea.

what we need to be, we need to be. the antarctic oracle,
the last permanent resident of the hotel splendide,
gives the only answer possible to every request for
    direction.

*

there are many old songs for warding off the evils of travel,
songs to calm the engines, songs in praise of railroad
    schedules,
lullabies that unleash your dreams in alien beds,

and little sestets to pacify the terror of what's left behind,
whose lines instruct you in the long, broken rhythms of
    passage.
their power lies in how you sing them to yourself, like this.

*

kiss me, says the oracle, i'm the best travel agent you'll
    ever find.
take my hand, says the inspector of customs, it is the
    custom here.
touch me, says the guide, i'll teach you how to pass as
    a native

and live in peace, here, in a simple hut, for ever after,
      with me.
well, this is a journey like no other journey we'll ever take:
best placate, within limits, the gods of travel. smile. say
      hello.

*

travel is so slow: each stage of the journey lasts a lifetime,
a dream from which we wake to pack our bags and rush
      to the station,
exhausted, falling asleep as soon as the train moves out,
      dreaming

both where can we go and not meet someone we knew
      long ago *and*
by the time we arrive in the land where we've always
      wanted to live
the people we wanted to live with there have gone
      somewhere else.

*

when we arrive in the city where no one crosses against
      the light,
where dogs step politely into the gutter and children
carry candy wrappers all day till they find a wastebasket,

when we step down from the plane onto the shiny asphalt
of human perfection . . . it is presumed we will know
      where we are

18

and behave accordingly. meanwhile, we're content to
      travel

among spies and smugglers, to smile easily at the corrupt
      and easy
smiles we meet at every border, the false bottom of our
      suitcase
packed with postcards from the tate, the louvre, the
      prado . . .

*

passionate travelogue: rising early we board the
      tongue-red bus
that guides us along the edges of the deep harbor, that
licks its way along the curving skyline drive. the city burns

while dali drifts over the lake in a soft balloon, sketching
turner in a dinghy in the harbor painting flames, painting
the stormy sunset on the red bus, the passionate tourists
      gaping.

*

in the dark, behind the storm, the slim figure of sex hovers
over me, unbuttoning my dreams, wrapping her long
      fingers
like mirrors around this hard, damp thing.

*

the postcard is the museum's exit to the outside world.
the back of the magritte is inscribed to the oracle:

19

some journey! what have you done to the people? to the
  walls?

the renoir goes to turner: here, someone for your harbor.
and this rousseau-like jungle scene, foliage dense with
  snow,
by the anonymous master of our dreams? we missed that:

let us return, for a while, to the gallery of possibilities.

*

see who it is who's touring this dream museum alone now,
humming a little song to himself to brave the dark
  passageways
winding north, steadily north. the coach that brought him

has driven away into the night, the servant who opened
  the green
door returned to his pose, peering over the doctor's
  shoulder
in 'the anatomy lesson,' poorly hung on the west wall high

above the cold fireplace. and he goes with one hand
  gliding
along the wet stone wall and the other ready to shield his
  face
when he sees what he sees in the garden at the end of the
  hall.

*

in the crowded municipal opera house we cannot identify
    ourselves.
the third who always walks beside us is us: oracle, guide
inspector of customs, wearing the badge that says, 'go
    north.'

4.

tourists languish on the grass, under heavy storm clouds,
      here
at the hard frontier of the north, expired passports on a
      dry lawn.
this impenetrable border not even rain passes through.
      not food or

passion: they starve who will not throw their whole lives
      upon it,
heeding the voice that says, cross this border, it's yours
      isn't it,
now's the time, you're ready, do it, push, harder, harder.
      i did.

*

beyond us lies another country. 'another country,'
      'another country.'
does anyone know what that means? there is, in the
      conservatory
beside the dream museum, an abstract egg-and-air plant
      whose roots

have roots that have roots that have roots that have
      roots. . . .
to begin to question it about its meaning is to begin
      everything:
to enter an intricate mirrormaze of schedules and passport
      photos.

*

how much further? we always ask. are we there yet?
    we're hungry.
we want to stretch our legs. where do we sleep tonight?
do we set our watches ahead now? what's that dark
    building?

isn't this where we always came on dream vacations?
nothing's changed, has it? we're really there now, aren't
    we?
what shall we do with our lives in a place like this?

*

north where the traffic is stalled at frozen intersections,
where we return from the airport to check the kitchen
    lights
and are abandoned by the last departing plane . . .
    where we'd live:

the tourists exude a tropic from behind their frosted
    windows,
a place to walk in the evening with cigar and expired
    passport,
to explore the erotic statuary discreetly arranged among
    the palms.

*

my dreams are full of fire when they are not full of water,
intricate pathways of the erotic north, where the wood is
    damp,

23

the chimney smokes, my line is always tangled with
      someone else's:

i am roughly awakened in the dark by a poem by 'lewis
      carroll,'
the 'ferocious passion' of its only remembered line blazing
with implication like the tidal wave that rises through
      my dream.

*

while this visit lasts we are at the center of the world. see:
the wind in the north, the red-winged blackbird in the
      south,
perched on a reed in the swamp in just that corner of the
      lake,

the center of the world in the thirty feet of water
      between us,
you there on the raft, i here on the dock. see: the very
      center
of the world between us, caught in a maze of iron-dark
      ripples.

*

the wind that sends the pine cones down like shrapnel
      from the trees,
the wind that moves the clouds that make the weather,
      the wind
that tears this piece of the north off the map of the
      world . . .

this wind that drives us into the passionate calm of our
      bodies
is always with us, noisy and inarticulate. if it drops, for
      an hour,
now, in the evening, that very silence is a pledge of its
      return.

*

the song of the sister draws the fragile voyager from his
      house,
the words at once enticing and forbidden, the music . . .
      well,
he uses up all his luminous renoir postcards, writing
      'sister,

. . . other times and other places,' rushes them south,
      and o,
rocked as he is in the arms of the erotic north, sister's a
      dream,
he has found his sister, sister's a dream, he has found . . .

*

we are amazed by the perfectly smooth brushwork of the
      overcast.
we are amazed by the wind, by the cold. finally we are
      amazed
at all the stars here. why can't we have skies like this at
      home?

*

in old-world cities where the mermaid still adorns the
        taverns,
drinkers ignore her golden breasts. the traveler never can,
who remembers, after all, the sober, sunlit reality of his
        own

half-naked lady on a raft in a lake at the north end of
        the world.

5.

is it time, now, for this journey to have some shape?
do we want more, now, than the anonymous whistle in
      the night
as the train slips down the mountain toward horseshoe
      bend?

are we bored with the echo of the foghorn from the dark
      harbor,
with the beginning of the descent to the foam-covered
      runway?
all right, then, let us decree we have arrived:

night-, snow-, storm-, and water-land. yes, we are here.
all the borders have been crossed. there are no secrets now.
what happens is enough. sometimes, more than enough.
      far more.

*

we enter our januaries like determined lovers, like travelers
whose lives are committed to the costliest off-season tours,
who *will* enjoy the hurricane season in miami, summer in
      sahara,

who understand, applaud, our willingness to travel north
      all year.
in this dream duluth stands for ice and possession. we move
to seize the most frigid times for travel: and make them
      ours.

*

we have met the coyote now, in winter dress in the empty
      field,
casting envious glances at the distant city. and his envy
is a weapon he would soon turn against us.

have we done wrong to visit the wild animal preserve in
      january?
it was meant as a 'highlight,' a 'museum without walls,'
but—guard! guard!—in the tall grass we cannot find the
      exit.

*

when we pull out the car, the highways are slick with ice.
the train sits in the station, the pass closed by a blizzard.
the airport is fogged in. the bus drivers are out on strike.

and the liners are locked for winter in the ice-bound
      harbor.

so we walk and it rains: in the woods, on the streets.
      wherever
we go like this is a place where we have been before.
      rejoice.

*

northern spring: the creek rises muddily over rusted
      tracks,
over the wheels of the stalled train, seeps through the
      coach floor

28

where the woman has taken the inspector of customs into
    her arms.

o see how someone else's art is everywhere, illuminated
through spring rain by reflections from these pale dream
    fires,
the lucid verso of these brief postcards from a modest
    exhibitionist.

*

how cool and safe the harbor where ice grips the shoreline
well into summer. do we know what fine place we are
    locked into?
it is july, august. 'the harbor is closed.' here we are.

*

we have traveled, traveled. been to the dark wood. to a
    darker one.
toured the labyrinthine harbor of duluth as if it were a
    work of art,
gone to the opera, camped on an island of animals that
    once were men

and dispersed them with our dreams: telling them each
    to each other
we have learned to overcome fear of the stranger, fear of
    the friend.
all this has brought us here: a long journey and a slow
    beginning!

29

*

classification of all places seen: conservatory, ice palace,
    desert,
harbor: how many images of the journey can be called
    up together?
never mind. what all these visitations have in common,
    what links

the wind and the red bus and the garden hung with
    mirrors, what
binds the oracle, the meadowlark, and the blackbird,
    what provides
some token clarity to earth's grand proliferation is . . .
    our life.

*

to move one—just one!—of these things is to rock the
    world.
with the wrong passengers the bus won't start. dali lets
    his pen
slip through his fingers and the picture darkens before
    it splashes

in the harbor waters far below. therefore we listen to the
    oracle,
who says, 'everything we come to as we travel can give
    us help.'
we come to everything: but only ourselves do we then
    move on.

*

there is one journey this journey the only journey,
        journey in/
to what we have been are and may and/or are yet to
        be, encompassed
by this spun, arcane, magnetic self. and because we do
        not know

the northwest passage *yet*, because the guide who takes
        us by the hand
has palms that sweat with indirection and every ticket
        is made out
in the name of possibility, we cannot stop until we
        reach the

PRINTED AT THE STINEHOUR PRESS, LUNENBURG, VERMONT